AIR SAFETY GROUP:

A BRIEF HISTORY

BY

J.W.RICKARD

First Edition: April 2010

Second Edition: May 2014

AIR SAFETY GROUP
(FOUNDED 1964)
WWW.AIRSAFETYGROUP.ORG

ISBN 978-1-291-87055-8

CONTENTS

FOREWORD

Air Safety Group

The Air Safety Group is needed as much today as it was when it was initiated 45 years ago by John Rickard, Frank Taylor and the late Robin Piercy. The international airline industry performs in the region of ten times more flights now than it did then. Yet today, despite such an enormous increase in traffic, there are fewer fatal accidents.

Those responsible for this remarkable achievement are the aviation industry's designers, manufacturers, suppliers, pilots, maintenance engineers, air traffic controllers, training establishments, government regulators, accident investigators, professional bodies and many others. They can all be proud of their collective achievement.

But complacency is always on the prowl, and too many accidents still happen as a result of forgotten lessons. This is where independent, expert analysis of accidents, incidents and trends helps to ensure that lessons are not lost.

The key word is independent. This has always been a principal qualification of the Air Safety Group, whose wide-ranging air safety expertise is independent, unpaid and impartial.

The Air Safety Group is a collective voice of everyone's prime objective.

J.M. (Mike) Ramsden
Editor of "Flight"1964-1981

February 2010

ACKNOWLEDGMENTS

My thanks are due to Mike Ramsden who kindly agreed to provide a foreword to this brief history. Although never a member, Mike has followed the progress of the Group from its inception to the present. The aviation press, and 'Flight' in particular, has always been more than ready to publicise the Group's position on various issues.

My thanks also to my co-founder, Frank Taylor, who has been continuously with the Group from its pre-formation days to the present. I have needed to consult Frank many times about various events, especially those which occurred during my very long absence from the Group.

Finally, my thanks are due to the several Group members who have provided material for inclusion in some of the sections of this history. Also to other members, past and present, whom I have consulted over details which have arisen in putting these few pages together. And to Robert and Karen Cooke who have undertaken the formatting of the history and making the necessary arrangements leading to its publication.

John Rickard

INTRODUCTION

Given that the 45th anniversary of the Group's formation occurred in December 2009, it has been felt appropriate to give an account of the circumstances leading to its formation and of its subsequent history up to the end of that year.

Other than reference to the jet fuel issue which brought the Group into being, and brief reference to a few other issues, no attempt is made in the body of this history to list the numerous items of concern which have exercised the Group during its 45 years of existence. Almost every issue affecting the safety of civil air transport has been discussed and many acted upon, actions taking the form of correspondence with the authorities (Dept for Transport, CAA, EASA, FAA) and with ICAO, meetings with the CAA, questions in Parliament, letters to the aviation press (in particular to Flight International) and the daily press, and correspondence with numerous associations and individuals.

Some of the Group's current concerns, mostly carried over from 2009, are referenced on the website which can be accessed at `http://www.airsafetygroup.org`. For the benefit of readers who do not have internet access, information on seven of these concerns is given as Appendix 1.

THE PRE-FORMATION ERA

The Group arose out of concern in the late fifties that some operators were understood to be using Jet B fuel on some sectors of their operations instead of the previously standard Jet A in their turbine-powered aircraft. Jet B was a more volatile fuel produced for military use[1], but it tended to be cheaper in some locations, hence providing a commercial incentive to use it. A number of people in the industry realised that this practice could eventually lead to loss of life in certain types of accident. Concern over the issue was strong amongst employees/former employees of de Havilland at Hatfield, in particular Robin Piercy, Frank Taylor and John Rickard, all of whom were working, or had worked, in the company's Powerplant Installation Department. These three, acting in a private capacity, formed the spearhead of an initiative launched to counter the move towards Jet B, this activity eventually leading to the formation of the Air Safety Group. (Note: in the early years the two fuels Jet A and Jet B were more widely known as kerosene (JP1) and wide-cut gasoline (JP4) respectively).

In the years leading up to 1960 there had been an exchange of correspondence with a number of airlines and other organisations. The outgoing letters would have been handwritten, copies of which are no longer available. Responses, however, from the various organisations are on file. There is an interesting exchange of correspondence with Trans Canada Airlines, the first operator to use Jet B. Concern amongst the engineers was increasing as further reports of Jet B usage were received.

Early in 1960 a significant event occurred in that Lord Brabazon, aviation pioneer and Chairman of the Air Registration Board, publicly expressed his concern, though without naming the 'offenders', about the increasing use of Jet B. In the summer of that year, Lord Brabazon returned to the subject, threatening

[1]Jet B was developed to provide maximum availability in the event of military conflict. Being of wider cut from the crude, larger quantities are available than is the case with Jet A.

to name the airlines concerned. The engineers were delighted to have such high level support, and contact between them and Lord Brabazon was established and continued until his death in 1964.

On 7 October, still in 1960, Lord Brabazon, through a letter in 'Flight', challenged the Jet B operators to a 'fuel duel': this was aimed at a number of foreign airlines whose preference for Jet B on economic grounds became evident at an IATA meeting in Copenhagen the previous month. On 11 November, there appeared, also in 'Flight', an authoritative but humorous letter from Robin Piercy, one of the founding engineers (though he wrote in a private capacity) proposing a 'fuel duel' which would demonstrate relative rates of flamespread and the proneness of Jet B to tank explosion. This letter caught the attention of the BBC which invited Piercy and Lord Brabazon to stage a demonstration for their 'Panorama' programme. In the event, Piercy was 'advised' by his company against participating, and so Rickard stepped in at short notice. The demonstration and broadcast took place on November 21 that year.

Lord Brabazon's campaign came to the attention of Sir Frank Whittle who, while feeling unable to become publicly involved, wrote to Lord Brabazon to assure him of his wholehearted moral support.

Early the following year (1961) Lord Brabazon initiated a debate on the subject in the House of Lords (Hansard 1 February 1961). This led to a Government inquiry into the relative safety of the two fuels. The inquiry reported in 1962 in favour of Jet A.

In 1962/63 Jet B usage was increasing. No regulatory authority saw fit to limit the practice, with the noteworthy exception of the then Australian Department of Civil Aviation. (It was not an issue in the UK as no British operator wished to use Jet B). Cynics pointed out that the trend was unlikely to be reversed until an accident occurred in which loss of life could fairly certainly be attributed to the use of this fuel. The first such accident occurred in December 1963[1], as a result of which it became evident that a group needed to be formally set-up to campaign on behalf of the safety of air travellers in this and other matters receiving insufficient attention from the industry and its regulatory authorities. The question arose: how to go about setting-up such a group? There were, of course, various associations for pilots, maintenance engineers, cabin crew, and the airline and manufacturing industries, some of which, through their technical committees, were doing well-researched work in the field of safety. Such associations, however, existed primarily for the benefit of their own mem-

[1]Pan Am B707 at Elkton, Maryland; December 8, 1963

bers. Nevertheless, the opinions of these and a variety of other organisations were sought concerning the foundation of a new group dedicated solely to the promotion of greater safety for air travellers. Much encouragement was received from James Tye, the controller of the British Safety Council (BSC). Tye made it clear, however, that the envisaged new group would not become part of the BSC.

On the assumption that the interest of members of Parliament would be advantageous, letters were sent to 12 MPs understood to be knowledgeable about aviation. Of replies received, two were worthy of note, one of which was from Eric Lubbock (Liberal) who expressed an interest in becoming involved in the proposed new group. Lubbock was a graduate engineer and had worked for Rolls-Royce before entering politics. The other initially encouraging response was from Fred Lee (Labour) who, for reasons now unclear, decided against joining. He did, however, engage in correspondence over the fuel issue with Julian Amery, the then Minister of Aviation. Amery responded with a useful letter clarifying the UK government's position on the issue[1].

In addition to the MPs, contact was made with numerous organisations and individuals, a number of whom expressed interest in the founding of the proposed group. One such individual worthy of mention is Harold Morris, a businessman who travelled extensively. He responded to a letter from Rickard which had been published in the Financial Times. Because of his valuable help, it was felt that the eventual group should always be open to laymen and not just to aviation professionals.

An ad hoc committee was set-up during the course of 1964, comprising Rickard, Piercy, Taylor, Morris, Lubbock, Tye and other interested individuals, this culminating in the Group's formation meeting.

---

[1]This letter indicated that, in the event of British operators contemplating changing to JET B, preventative regulatory action would be considered.

THE FORMATION MEETING AND DIFFICULTIES ENCOUNTERED UP TO MID-1968

The formation meeting was held at the Royal Aero Club on December 8 1964, though sadly without Lord Brabazon who had died earlier that year. Eric Lubbock and Harold Morris were elected joint Chairmen, and John Rickard as Honorary Secretary. Nine organisations were represented at the meeting, the minutes of which are given in Appendix 2. These minutes do not make clear the total number of founder members. For the record, they were Earnest Bass, Nancy Cox, John Lodge, Eric Lubbock MP, Harold Morris, Robin Piercy, Dr Frank Preston, John Rickard, Frank Taylor, Basil Townshend, James Tye and David Wakeling. (Lubbock, Preston and Townshend were unable to attend the meeting).

It must be emphasised that not all the individuals and organisations listed in the minutes joined the Group. Furthermore it is not clear in retrospect whether, and to what extent, any of the organisations present were expected to become officially associated after the formation meeting. It soon became evident, however, that association with other organisations could compromise the main objectives of the Group. For this reason the Group's association with the British Safety Council was amicably terminated.

Although the formation meeting was held at the Royal Aero club, and occasional meetings have been held at other venues, the House of Commons became the principal meeting place until 2007. This privilege was arranged by Eric Lubbock, founder member and first joint chairman. (He later served for several years as Vice-President following his accession, as Lord Avebury, to the Upper House).

As Eric Lubbock was a Liberal MP, and as at the time of writing this history the Group's parliamentary member, Tom Brake, is a Liberal Democrat, the impression might be given that the Group has an official linkage with the Liberal Democrat party. This would be an incorrect assumption. The Group has no formal link with any political party or indeed with Parliament at all. For much of the Group's history, its later members in the Commons have been Conservatives, namely, Norman (now Lord) Tebbit, the late Sir Michael McNair Wilson, and John Wilkinson. The Group's current President, the hereditary Conservative peer, Lord Gainford, has also been very active on the Group's behalf. So far as the Labour party is concerned, the Group has had no Labour members of the Lower House on its strength, but has had two Labour members of the Upper House, namely, Lord Stoddart of Swindon and the late Lord Beswick, both of whom served as Group Presidents.

The Group has always respected the desire for anonymity on the part of certain of its members. For this reason, not all members' names are referred to in this history although several such members have made significant contributions to the Group's activities.

As already recounted, it was a Jet B-related fatal accident in December 1963 which provided the final impetus leading to the Group's formation. In addition, a further Jet B-related fatal accident occurred in 1964[1] just three weeks prior to formation. The first major task therefore was to provide a substantial input to the controversy surrounding these two accidents, especially as the Federal Aviation Administration (FAA) had, following the first of these accidents, initiated an enquiry[2] into the relative safety of the two fuels. The Group set-up a working party to review these matters and to put together a definitive report, "A Review of the Aviation Fuel Controversy" which was issued in December 1966. The report went through several drafts before publication: in addition it was deemed desirable to have it vetted by legal experts for possible libelous statements. (Some retrospective comment on this report together with up-to-date information related to fuel system safety could make a worthwhile addendum to the original).

[1]TWA B707 at Rome; November 23, 1964

[2]This enquiry had been sub-contracted to the Co-Ordinating Research Council. The Council's findings were reported by the FAA in January 1965 to the effect that there was no substantial difference between the two fuels from the standpoint of safety. These findings were in conflict with those of the UK Government report already referred to. In 1973, however, the FAA requested the Council to update its earlier report in the light of more recently acquired data. The updated report concluded that Jet A is safer than Jet B in accidents on or near the airport, and in the flight and ground servicing modes.

Within a few weeks, both of the Group's formation and of the second Jet B-related accident referred to above, the US operators involved in the two accidents announced that they were abandoning the use of Jet B. This was very good news, although a number of non-US operators continued for a while with Jet B. Much credit for the improved situation goes to the American-founded Airways Club. A cordial liaison had been established with the Club which had been responsible for publicising in the US the activities of Rickard and Lord Brabazon on the fuel issue.

The Airways Club was concerned not only with safety, as already noted, but with several other aspects of air travel of interest to its members, e.g. hotel and car bookings, and insurance. Its President was David Quinn, a former US Navy pilot. As the Club had only a few UK members, Quinn approached the newly formed Air Safety Group with a proposal which argued that the interest of safety would be better served if the Group's and the Club's activities in the UK could be brought together in a new organisation, Airways Club Ltd, in which Rickard would be invited to become an officer. This interesting proposal was discussed amongst the officers, but courteously declined. So many of the Group's members were single-minded engineers concerned solely with safety, and who would prefer not to have to become involved with matters such as bookings and insurance. The Airways Club later reformed itself into the Airline Passengers Association, and eventually as the International Airline Passengers Association.

As has been stated already, the Group's three principal founding engineers were employees of de Havilland at Hatfield. In 1956 Rickard left de Havilland and spent the following 12 years with two other companies, both of which took a benign view of his air safety activities. Taylor also left de Havilland to take up a post with an accessory company which, as in Rickard's case, raised no objection to his private safety activities. Taylor later embarked on a long career at the College of Aeronautics (later Cranfield University) which guaranteed him a degree of academic freedom. Piercy, although spending two relatively short periods with other companies, remained for many years in a senior capacity at the Hatfield site. He was able to continue as a Group member, while avoiding public involvement in contentious issues.

In 1968 Rickard wished to return to the mainstream of the aircraft construction industry, and accordingly took up a post with one of the main constructors (British Aircraft Corporation, Weybridge). Being aware that he had contributed a number of letters and articles in the press, his new employer felt that there could be some conflict of interest. They therefore requested that he should relinquish his membership of the Group. Although disappointed, Rickard was understanding of the company's concern. He rejoined the Group on retirement 23 years later.

This issue of potential conflict of interest probably deterred a number of otherwise well qualified people from joining. A particularly interesting case is that of Dr Frank Preston, a founder member. Preston was at that time BEA's Deputy Director of Medical Services. Shortly after the Group's formation, Rickard received a courteously worded letter from the corporation's Chief Executive saying that he had requested Dr Preston not "to participate directly" in the Group's work. Many years later, following amalgamation of the two state corporations, Preston felt able to resume his active participation. He eventually became Medical Director of British Airways and was a renowned authority on aviation medicine. He was awarded an OBE for services to aviation and was later to become a GAPAN Liveryman.

By contrast, another doctor who was involved with the Group in its early days felt able to continue without restraint. He was Dr Kenneth Bergin, the Chief Medical Officer of BOAC, a Liveryman and former Master of GAPAN. He served the Group with distinction for many years in the capacities of Deputy Chairman and President.

In the weeks leading up to Rickard's departure, an appraisal was made of the Group's activities in the three and a half years since formation. Clearly, some early aspirations had not been achieved, though this was due mainly to the considerable effort that was required to cover the fuel controversy. There was still no formal membership, nor was there a constitution although a statement of aims had been made available to enquirers. On the positive side it must be stated that the Group's fuel report was very well received, having been widely distributed. Also, contact had been made with many people who were grateful for the Group's expertise.

One of the issues of concern to the Group then (as now) was flight time limitations. This matter was researched by Nancy Cox, a founder member and former flight attendant. She produced a draft report which was highly commended by one of the Group's medical advisers but which, for some reason now unknown, was not issued. Amongst other topics of concern was the then lack of legal protection of cabin staff against excessive working hours. Mrs Cox headed a small working party which issued in June 1967 a short report highlighting this situation, "Cabin Staff and Air Safety".

Rickard left the Group in the spring of 1968, thus creating a vacancy for the Honorary Secretaryship. This was filled by Frank Taylor who was just settling into his new job at the College of Aeronautics. In the course of his career at the College/Cranfield University, he continued to specialise in aircraft systems and later, in addition, cabin safety and accident investigation, becoming Director of the Cranfield Aviation Safety Centre. He is a Fellow of ISASI, and in 1998 received the Jerome Lederer award. Taylor remains a member of the Group, having served as Honorary Secretary, Chairman and Honorary Treasurer.

One of the administrative difficulties, never wholly resolved, was the lack of a permanent Group address. Being neither a company nor charity the Group has had no registered address. For a relatively short period after formation, the Group was able to use the address of the British Safety Council as a forwarding address. Eventually it was accepted that the address would be the private addresses of the various secretaries or chairmen, as appropriate.

OFFICERS AND PARLIAMENTARY MEMBERS FROM MID-1968

Following Rickard's departure a number of changes occurred. Morris stood down from the joint Chairmanship but remained a committee member. Lubbock continued as Chairman. At the same time, Dr Bergin was elected Deputy Chairman. Taylor was confirmed as the Honorary Secretary and he also took on the additional role of Honorary Treasurer[1].

The matter of a Group constitution had been addressed, and a final version was issued in August 1968. The initial membership subscription was set at £1 p.a.

Unfortunately for the Group, Lubbock failed to retain his parliamentary seat in the general election in June 1970. In the circumstances he felt unable to continue as chairman, though he later maintained his Group interest in the capacity of Vice-President. Meanwhile, the Group had been joined by Norman Tebbit who had been elected a member of Parliament, having retired from BOAC as a pilot. His aviation expertise and his presence in the Commons enabled the Group's influence to continue to be felt in that arena.

Surprisingly, the Group had not held a formal Annual General Meeting until late 1970, the first such being held on December 3 that year.

Following the resignation of Lubbock as Chairman, meetings were chaired by stopgap chairmen until late February 1971 at which time Tebbit took over the Chairmanship. Later the same year, Dr Bergin stood down from the Deputy Chairmanship and was appointed as the Group's first President. Basil Townshend, a Group founder member, was elected Deputy Chairman.

---

[1]For reasons unclear, the position of Honorary Treasurer, together with the name of the holder, was not added to the Group's headed paper until 1977. Taylor retained the position throughout his time as Secretary, and then Chairman, and for many years after.

It is worth mentioning briefly that 1973 saw a resurrection of the jet fuel issue, this on account of the world oil crisis that year, which resulted in a temporary shortage of Jet A fuel at some locations. The matter was eventually satisfactorily resolved.

At the AGM in 1973, Basil Townshend stood down from the Deputy Chairmanship, his place being taken by Lt Cdr C J Howe RN. Cdr Howe had joined the Group in 1970, having been introduced by Townshend.

In February 1975 Tebbit indicated his wish to stand down after serving four years as Chairman, this on account of his increasing parliamentary work load, part of which had to do with reviewing the Labour Government's bill to nationalise the aircraft construction industry. After a few weeks, Taylor was elected Chairman. Cdr Howe stood down from the Deputy Chairmanship, his place being taken by Tebbit. Anna Mackenzie, a qualified nurse and former flight attendant, took over Taylor's previous duties as Secretary.

In December 1975 the death of Basil Townshend was announced. Townshend had been one of the earliest and most active members during the Group's formative years. One of the RAeS's awards (escape and rescue) is named after him.

In February 1977, after two years as Chairman, Taylor felt obliged to relinquish the position on account of his professional workload at Cranfield University. This highlighted the difficulty of finding suitably qualified people to fill the principal posts within the Group. A Group member, Capt Bressey, volunteered to approach a recently retired BA Captain and colleague who, he felt, would be well suited to take on the Chairmanship. As a result of this approach, Capt Eric Pritchard, a GAPAN Liveryman, was brought into the Group, quickly becoming elected as Chairman. This brought about a long, stable period under Pritchard's Chairmanship which continued for fifteen years.

As a result of the general election in 1979, and the return of a Conservative administration, Tebbit felt obliged to resign from the Group on account of his increased political responsibilities. Later that year, Michael McNair-Wilson MP joined the Group, becoming Deputy Chairman, thus ensuring the continued presence of a member of the Lower House.

In April 1980. Anna Mackenzie, the Group's Secretary, resigned on health grounds. Her place was taken by Erica Knights who continued as Secretary until October 1983.

The death of the Group's President, Dr Bergin, was announced early in 1981, the position remaining vacant until Lord Beswick, a former BOAC pilot, came into the Group the following year.

In July 1983 the Group was joined by John Boulding MBE, recently retired from British Airways as Chief Air Safety Investigator. He had been awarded an MBE for services to aviation safety. He was a member of ISASI and in 1980 was a recipient of the Jerome Lederer award. In December he took over the Secretaryship following the resignation of Erica Knights.

Late in 1984 Lord Beswick resigned as President, leaving a vacancy which was not filled for a year and a half.

In April 1986, Lord Stoddart of Swindon joined the Group as President.

During the lead-up to the AGM held in February 1992, both Pritchard and Boulding announced that they would not be standing for re-election. Rickard had recently rejoined the Group after an absence of 23 years: he was shortly to retire from British Aerospace where he was a Principal Airworthiness Engineer.

At the AGM Walter Lynch and John Rickard were elected Chairman and Hon Secretary respectively. Taylor remained as Hon Treasurer. Lynch had joined the Group in 1987 and was currently running his own business, having retired from a career in the RAF as an Engineer Officer. McNair Wilson (now Sir Michael) announced that he would not be seeking re-election to Parliament at the forthcoming general election. He agreed to approach John Wilkinson MP who he felt, if re-elected, would be well suited to stand for the Deputy Chairmanship.

In June 1992 Wilkinson attended his first Group meeting, having been re-elected as member for Northwood and Ruislip. He had an aviation background, having served as a pilot in the Royal Air Force.

Also in 1992, Lord Stoddart stood down from his position as President. Lord Avebury was approached regarding this position, but felt unable to accept on account of his parliamentary and business commitments. The position of President remained vacant until in 1994 when one of the Group's pilot members, Sydney Lane, introduced to the Group a wartime RAF colleague, Lord Gainford, a hereditary peer. Lord Gainford was quickly elected to the Presidency, thus re-establishing a Group presence in the Upper House. (See later under 'ASG Membership')

Regrettably, on account of his parliamentary duties, John Wilkinson, stood down from the Deputy Chairmanship in 1995, thus leaving the Group temporarily without a member in the Commons. This posed a problem concerning room bookings within the Palace of Westminster. Lord Gainford was able to assist in this matter by arranging for some of the Group's regular meetings to be held in the House of Lords. Later in the year the Group's chairman made contact with a former RAF colleague, Keith Mans MP. While Mr Mans was sympathetic towards the Group's objectives, he felt that, on account of his parliamentary duties, he would be unable to become active on the Group's behalf. He undertook, however, to arrange room bookings for the Group's regular meetings. This arrangement continued until the general election in 1997.

A further change in 1995 was the election of Peter Webb as Honorary Treasurer, taking over from Frank Taylor who had held the position for 27 years. Webb, who had joined the Group in 1971, had earlier been on the academic staff of Cranfield University, specialising in computer studies.

In 1996 the death of Robin Piercy was announced. He was one of the original three founder members of the Group.

At the general election in 1997 Keith Mans failed to be re-elected, thus depriving the Group of its privilege of holding meetings in the Commons. The Institution of Mechanical Engineers therefore became the temporary venue until further support could be solicited from members of Parliament. As the Group's spokesmen had for 21 years been from the Conservative benches, and as no Labour member appeared to be available, it was decided that an approach should be made to be Liberal Democrats, bearing in mind that, as recorded earlier in this account, a Liberal member, Eric Lubbock (now Lord Avebury), was a founder member and former joint Chairman of the Group. This approach elicited a generous response from the Liberal Democrats and resulted in Tom Brake MP, a physics graduate (Imperial College), becoming, in the spring of 1998, the Group's parliamentary member.

In early 1999 Walter Lynch expressed his wish to stand down from the Chairmanship, having completed seven years in the post. Accordingly, at the AGM in February that year, Group Capt John Tritton AFC was elected Chairman. He had joined the Group some two and a half years earlier, having previously been Technical Director and then Clerk to GAPAN of which he was a Liveryman. He had also been a Chairman of the UKFSC. At the same AGM, Peter Webb stood down from the Treasurership for health reasons and was replaced by Frank Taylor.

At the 2000 AGM Rickard stood down from the Secretaryship, having completed eight years in the post. He was then elected Deputy Chairman, a position that had been vacant for several years. It is not clear why this position had not been filled earlier. By tradition the post had been occupied by a member of Parliament but, in view of the difficulty parliamentary members sometimes experienced in attending Group meetings, current thinking was that the post should preferably be filled by an ordinary Group member.

Consequent upon Rickard standing down as Secretary, Capt Russ Williams was elected to the post. Capt Williams had an extensive helicopter background and first joined the Group in 1979. He had, however, relinquished his membership in 1987 on joining the Civil Aviation Authority with which he became Head of Flight Operations Policy and Regulations. He rejoined the Group in 1998 on retirement. Capt Williams is a GAPAN Liveryman and a member of ISASI.

At the 2001 AGM Capt Williams relinquished the secretarial post on account of pressure of his consultancy work. Rickard returned as Secretary in an acting capacity.

At the 2002 AGM George Maloney was elected as Secretary. He had joined the Group in 2001 and was currently employed by an aircraft maintenance company. However, he felt unable to continue in the secretarial post for more than a year on account of pressure of his professional work.

At the 2003 AGM there were no nominations for the Secretaryship, and the Chairman felt obliged to suspend the normal meetings until a new Secretary could be found. Nevertheless some less formal meetings took place.

Later in 2003 the death occurred of Dr Frank Preston, a founder member and prominent contributor to the Group's medical activities

At the 2004 AGM Dr Graham Braithwaite, a newly-joined member, was elected as Secretary. Dr Braithwaite is Director of the Cranfield Safety and Accident Investigation Centre, and is a member of ISASI. Like his two predecessors in the post, however, he was experiencing difficulty in continuing, and George Maloney returned as acting Secretary for the remainder of the year.

Also at the 2004 AGM, Rickard stood down from the Deputy Chairmanship. He was replaced by Tony Wassell who had joined the Group in 2001. At his retirement, Wassell had been the Chief Airworthiness Engineer of Rolls-Royce. He was a recipient of the Royal Aeronautical Society's Wakefield Gold Medal for services to aviation safety.

During the course of 2004, Frank Taylor relinquished the Treasurership. He was replaced by Robert Cooke, a Cranfield graduate (Air Transport) who was currently employed in airport management. He had joined the Group in 2001.

At the 2005 AGM George Maloney felt able to commit to a further period as Secretary and was duly elected.

The above paragraphs reveal the difficulty the Group experienced for some years over the Secretaryship. The demands of the post had proven unduly onerous for members in full time employment or engaged in consultancy work.

At the AGM in April 2006, Group Capt Tritton stood down from the Chairmanship and retired from the Group. Capt Williams was elected as Chairman.

Prior to the AGM in 2007, George Maloney had expressed a desire to stand down from the Secretaryship, again on account of pressure of his full-time work. Accordingly, Robin Boning was elected to the position. He had joined the Group the previous year, having retired from the CAA with which he had served for many years as a Powerplant Installation Design Surveyor.

At the AGMs in 2008 and 2009, the Group's officers remained as above.

RETROSPECTIVE

Has the Group Been Worthwhile?

This history has so far chronicled the events leading to the Group's formation together with some of the problems encountered in the early years. The names of the Group's officers and some other members up to the present have been given in narrative form.

The question inevitably arises: has the Group achieved anything in its forty-five years, and has the effort expended been worthwhile? The Group is confident in asserting that the successful resolution of the Jet A/Jet B fuel issue prevented the loss of many lives, though this may not have been achieved without the powerful assistance of the then Airways Club. The jet fuel issue was of a unique type, other issues being much less clear-cut and their outcomes more difficult to quantify. As already stated in the introduction, almost every issue affecting the safety of civil air transport has been discussed, some at great length, and many acted upon.

On the negative side it is easier to state what the Group has not achieved rather than what it has: for example, only two reports were ever published, and those in the very early days. Other reports were being worked on but never reached publication. At this distance in time it is not possible to account for this, other than to record the fact that the authors of the intended reports were very busy in their professional lives.

The Group is concerned solely with the safety of civil air travellers, and is independent of commercial pressures. It embraces a range of expertise embracing operations, engineering, medicine and accident investigation. The existence of such a monitoring group has, almost by definition, made it a worthwhile enterprise.

Nevertheless, notwithstanding the merits referred to above, and having regard to the complexity of the current aviation scene, a thoroughgoing review of the Group's structure and mode of operation was undertaken earlier in the present decade. A number of changes were implemented with a view to increasing the fitness of the Group to meet the challenges which lay ahead.

Group Funding

In view of the Group's expertise, the privilege of holding its meetings in the Palace of Westminster, and of being addressed by many prominent specialists, the question arises: why is the Group not better known to the aviation public? The answer would appear to lie in its lack of adequate funding and hence its inability to mount seminars. This potential problem was identified very early by Dr Bergin, one of the Group's most distinguished members. At its outset the founding engineers felt, somewhat idealistically, that communication with the regulatory authorities and other bodies would in itself be sufficient to advance the Group's objectives. They had failed to realise the importance of addressing the wider aviation community.

The Group is funded almost wholly by the subscriptions of its members. As the subscription at its foundation was £1 p.a, and is currently £20 p.a. it will be appreciated that the Group's income can do little more than pay administration and miscellaneous expenses. A recent scan through the records reveals three 'no strings' donations, namely £100 and £50 from equipment manufacturers, and £100 from a national newspaper. Time and again the Group's chairmen and other members, drawing attention to the lack of funding, proposed various ways of attracting donations. None succeeded. The most recent to be investigated was the possibility of obtaining a grant from the National Lottery, but this, for various reasons, was abandoned.

The largest boost to the Group's finances occurred, totally unexpectedly, in 2001 as a result of the termination of a will trust. One of the Group's members, who died many years previously, had left a small legacy. But, unbeknown to the Group, a further, much larger, sum became potentially available, having been tied into a will trust that terminated on the death of his widow which occurred many years later. This sum provided an approximate fourfold increase in the Group's bank balance. The means were then available to mount at least one or more full day events. Accordingly the Group's medical members set up a seminar on the subject of drugs and alcohol and the dangers of these substances in the aviation context. Prominent speakers in the field were engaged and the event was to be held at a prestigious location. There followed a cruel irony: the tickets were not selling well enough, and the Group felt obliged to cancel the event in order to cut its losses.

Clearly, not withstanding the technical expertise contained within the Group, there was insufficient business acumen to attract adequate funding.

With hindsight, the Group's objectives may have been better served had it accepted, at the outset, the then Airways Club's offer to have it become incorporated into an Airways Club Ltd, although, as already noted, this would have involved taking on issues in addition to safety.

The Regulatory Scene

At the time of the ASG's formation, civil aviation safety was regulated, as now, by the Civil Aviation Act, the main provisions for day-to-day reference being set forth in the Air Navigation Order(CAP 393). Technical and safety standards relating to design, construction and maintenance were delegated to the Air Registration Board (ARB) and published in British Civil Airworthiness Requirements (BCAR). Certain functions, however, were retained by the responsible government department, the then Board of Trade (BoT). Certificates of airworthiness were granted by the BoT on the recommendation of the ARB. The BoT retained certain other functions, e.g. operational matters including the overseeing of operations by foreign registered aircraft when in the UK.

A major change in the above scene occurred in April 1972 with the formation of the Civil Aviation Authority (CAA) in accordance with the recommendations of the Edwards Report. This new delegated authority replaced the ARB, taking over the latter's responsibilities plus responsibility for operational matters formerly exercised by the BoT. Certificates of Airworthiness would henceforth be issued by the new authority. As previously, however, the BoT and its successor departments retained responsibility for foreign airline operations in the UK.

At the CAA's formation, a presentation on the new authority was held at Lancaster House. This was attended by the Group's then Honorary Secretary, Frank Taylor.

Following on from collaboration between the UK and France in producing a code of requirements (TSS) for supersonic aircraft (namely Concorde and possible derivatives), a number of European constructors were expressing concern over a lack of harmonised standards for certification of new European subsonic aircraft (e.g. the forthcoming A300 and other types). Accordingly these constructors and their respective national authorities collaborated to produce a set of requirements which became known as the Joint Airworthiness Requirements (JAR) ('Airworthiness' later being changed to 'Aviation'). The overseeing body for this process consisted of the major national authorities acting collectively as the Airworthiness Authorities Steering Group (AASG): more Authorities were invited to join in this process and adopt JARs as their national codes. This was formalised by the signing in 1979 of the first 'Arrangements', with the signatory States becoming known collectively as the Joint Airworthiness Authorities (JAAs). Although the requirements were 'joint', their implementation was left to each individual State. With a view to potential sales to the United States, the new European large aircraft requirements were based mainly on those of the Federal Aviation Administration, but initially with many National Variants requested by some European Authorities included in the text. The first codes to be accepted by the CAA were JAR 25 which, for new types, replaced BCAR Section D (Design Requirements for Large Aircraft); and JAR-E which, for engines, replaced the requirements of BCAR Section C (Engines & Propellers). Other JAR codes were introduced progressively.

During the latter part of the 1980s, the European Authorities had removed all National Variants from JAR 25 and signed, in 1989, a further set of agreements ('the Cyprus agreements'). These formally brought into being the Joint Aviation Authorities (JAA) and required all signatories to adopt JARs as their sole national codes.

At about this time the European Union was taking an increasing interest in the regulation of aviation safety, and in 1991 published EC Regulation 3922/91 which made certain sections of JAR mandatory within all member States. Furthermore, it effectively prohibited unilateral changes by any member State in respect of any of the matters covered by the mandatory sections of JAR. The ASG was profoundly disturbed by the implications of this new regulation, feeling that its provisions ran counter in certain instances to the quest for improved safety standards. For example, following the Boeing 737 accident at Manchester in 1985, the CAA sponsored research into emergency evacuation to be carried out by Cranfield University. One recommendation arising from this research was that the minimum permitted passageway width through bulkheads leading to emergency exits be increased. The CAA was in favour of this recommendation and was expected to make it applicable to all UK-registered public transport aircraft. However, 3922/91 prevented the CAA from adopting it unless and until such time as all the EU national authorities were in agreement. At the time of writing, 23 years after Manchester, it has still not been adopted. The ASG accepts that the ideal is for all EU States to move together in the interest of harmonisation, but where this cannot be achieved, it has advocated that unilateral action be permitted by any member State to introduce safety features which are in advance of those obtaining in the other States.

As the 1990s moved on, it became clear that the multi-authority regulatory arrangements lacked a sufficient legal basis for an expanding European Union: furthermore these arrangements presented difficulties in negotiating type certificate validations with the FAA. This realisation brought about a fundamental regulatory change with the formation in 2003 of the European Aviation Safety Agency (EASA) which, as a single authority, would eventually take over many of the functions of the national authorities together with the rule-making function of the JAA. Through the European Commission, EASA would develop its own technical requirements, based for the most part on existing JARs.

While the ASG concedes that the idealistic stance advocated prior to the formation of EASA may not, on account of the drive for harmonisation, be realisable, it remains concerned that some dilution of UK standards could occur under the EASA system. Whilst currently, for example, the UK Flight and Duty Time Limitations (CAP 371 4th Edition) is permitted to continue as a derogation within the UK, it will be superseded in 2012 by EU OPS Subpart Q which came into force within the other EU States in July 2008. The ASG does not think this scheme is fit for purpose as currently written, particularly in view of the lack of implementation of the recommendations in the Moebus Aviation Scientific and Medical review that took place towards the end of 2008.

Reference should be made to the ASG website for other comments and concerns arising from the EASA system.

ASG Membership

The Group currently has 25 members. Traditionally, membership has been maintained by invitation from existing members. In early 2001, however, feeling that a modest increase in number would be desirable, a brief notice about the Group was printed, courtesy of the editor, in the RAeS's 'Aviation Professional'. This brought about a surprising response, indicating considerable interest within the wider aviation constituency. Several of those who enquired joined, bringing in further expertise in the fields of operations, certification, maintenance engineering, and airport management. With a number of older members retiring from active membership, this approach was repeated in 2007. Again, considerable interest was evoked, resulting in an influx of expertise in various disciplines including air traffic management and aircraft maintenance.

It is a matter of regret that there are at present no women members, although several made valuable contributions, both technically and secretarially, in the earlier years. One, not so far mentioned, is Capt Yvonne Sintes who achieved two 'firsts' in British aviation. She was the first woman to become a Ministry of Aviation air traffic controller, much of her time in this capacity being at Gatwick airport. Later in her career, having become a professional pilot, she was the first woman to command turbine-powered aircraft (HS 748 & BAC 1-11) in public transport operations. Capt Sintes was the recipient in 1974 of the Whitney Straight award[1].

Membership of the Group has comprised a mix mostly of retired aviation professionals and others still in employment. Ideally, a larger proportion of the latter category would be desirable, though unattainable on account of the conflict-of-interest issue referred to earlier in this account. Membership has also included a small number of laymen with interest in aviation affairs.

The names of the Group's officers and parliamentary members, up to the present, have already been given. The committee, however, comprises the officers together with elected/co-opted members. This latter category currently includes Capt Chris Roberts who joined the Group in 2001. Capt Roberts, formerly of British Aerospace (military) and My Travel International Airways was a recipient of a GAPAN medal and also of the R.P Alston Medal (RAeS), both for services to test flying. Also David Haward who joined the Group in 2007, having, earlier, spent 30 years with the CAA from which he retired as Deputy Chief Surveyor. Following retirement he worked for ICAO in Montreal for two years on training issues and also human factors arising in aircraft maintenance. He is currently a consultant to several operators.

While names of officers and parliamentary members have always been given on the Group's headed notepaper, for some years the names of other members and their specialities were also included on the notepaper and were thus in the public domain.

Reference to former members, however, is constrained by the possible desire of some not to be named. In view of the 45 year existence of the Group, some members will have died, and others, through loyalty to former employers, may still be reluctant to be named. It may not be practicable at this stage to obtain

[1]This award was established in 1967 by Mr Whitney Straight to recognise the achievement and status of women in aviation.

their retroactive consent.

Given the above constraint, the names of some other former members are given in the following paragraph.

Of such members, mention is due to Dr Ian Hill OBE, a pathologist prominent in the field of accident survival; to John Lodge DFC, a Group founder member and formerly the CAA's Chief Fire Service Officer; to Sydney Lane, Phil Branson DFM, Capts Skelt, Palmer, Bressey, Insole and Morton, all formerly of British Airways and its predecessor corporations; to Dr Sowby who specialised in risk assessments; to Hugh Field, a GAPAN Liveryman and former Master of the Guild whose interests encompassed pilot training and aviation journalism with particular reference to operations; and to Dr Horsfall who special interest was emergency evacuation.

Of current Group members of long standing, mention is due to two to whom reference has already been made. Firstly to Lord Gainford, the Group's President, who had been most active in raising matters of aviation concern in the Lords. Regrettably, Lord Gainford, along with most other hereditary peers, lost his right to a seat in the Lords as a result of the House of Lords Act 1999. Secondly, to parliamentary member Tom Brake for his many activities in the Commons on behalf of the Group, and to his constituency office for arranging room bookings for the Group's meetings. Mention is also due to Stephen Barlay, Patrick Forman and Maurice Allward for their very long membership, all of whom have written books on aviation; to Robert Belton, formerly with British Airways, retiring as Assistant Air Safety Adviser, and recipient in 1975 of the Douglas Weightman Award for services to air safety, and, in 1982, of the IATA Safety Advisory Award; to Dr Kenneth Edgington, formerly Chief Medical Officer of the CAA, currently consultant in occupational and aviation medicine, and a GAPAN Liveryman; to Capt Ian Frow, a GAPAN Liveryman who had formerly been Training Standards Captain with British Airways and later Training Captain with Virgin Atlantic; and to Andrew Weir, aviation author and producer of aviation safety documentaries for television.

More recently-joined members include Ronald Ashford (whose untimely death in occurred in 2008), Phil Burgess (maintenance engineering), Terry Davies (airworthiness/human factors), Andrew du Boulay (air traffic management), Capt John Hoyte (Cabin Air Quality), Stuart Mackrell and John Sawyer (maintenance engineering).

Meeting Venues

References have already been made to the fact that the Group's principal meeting place, from its inception, had been the House of Commons. In more recent years some meetings had also been held in Portcullis House and two other locations within the parliamentary estate. Other venues have included the Institution of Mechanical Engineers, and, through the good offices of Chairman, Group Capt Tritton, the Guild of Air Pilots and Air Navigators

In 2005, however, the Office of the Parliamentary Commissioner for Standards issued a booklet entitled "Guide to the Rules on All-Party Groups". The purpose of this was to remind MPs and others of the rules governing the make-up of groups which held, or wished to hold, their meetings within the parliamentary estate. The rules derived from two Resolutions made by the House of Commons in 1984 and 1985. In view of these rules, the Group's parliamentary member, Tom Brake, felt obliged to inform the Group that, as constituted, it would no longer be able to enjoy the privilege of meeting within the estate.

In order to continue meeting in the Commons and Portcullis House, the Group's name would need to be added to the All-Party Groups' Register: this would require that the Group should have at least two officers, all of whom must be members of the Commons or Lords (with at least one from the Commons). To achieve a higher status, the Group would need to apply for entry to the "Approved List" of All-Party Parliamentary Groups: this would require 20 qualifying members from the Commons or Lords, this number comprising 10 from the Government party plus 10 from the Opposition/Other parties. Clearly the second of these two options was quite unattainable, even should it be considered desirable. Regarding the first option, the Group had many times felt that a modest increase in its parliamentary members would be advantageous, though it never succeeded in having more than two (Commons and Lords) at any one time. However, it was felt that for parliamentarians to fill all the officer posts would unacceptably alter the character of the Group.

Critics of the ASG have sometimes asserted that the Group is 'too political', though without saying precisely what they meant. The Group has always stated that it is strictly non-party political and, furthermore, that it has no formal parliamentary connection. A search through the archives, however, reveals two occasions on which a member has incorrectly referred to the Group as the "All Party Parliamentary Air Safety Group". This indicates that there has from time to time been some confusion over the Group's status. Meeting minutes record that Deputy Chairman, Sir Michael McNair Wilson MP, raised the matter of the

Group's status in 1987, but stated that the Group could continue as it had always done, if it so wished.

It is a matter of speculation as to how the Group was able to meet within the estate for so long largely untroubled by the above considerations. Such rules as existed were presumably less precise than the current ones. The Group's presence occurred firstly by invitation from its first parliamentary member and founder member, Eric Lubbock (Lord Avebury), this establishing a precedent which was upheld by the succeeding parliamentary members. The Group is grateful for the privilege of having been being able to meet within the estate for more than forty years.

Currently the Group's main meeting venue is the Institution of Mechanical Engineers.

Group Anniversaries

On achieving its first 20 years, a statement was submitted to the technical press to mark the event and to invite interested readers to contact the Group. On reaching its 30th anniversary, however, it was felt fitting to mark the event with a gathering at the House of Commons which was hosted jointly by Deputy Chairman, John Wilkinson MP, and Chairman Walter Lynch. This was attended by 49 members/former members and guests. The proceedings were concluded with a tour of the House.

The 40th anniversary was marked with a similar event, this time being hosted jointly by the Group's parliamentary member, Tom Brake, and Chairman Group Capt Tritton. Some 38 members/former members and guests attended. Again, the proceedings were concluded with a tour of the House.

Group Archives and Communications

A large amount of archival material covering the period extending from the pre-formation days to the present is available, mainly in hard copy. There are, however, some gaps in the record, these probably having arisen on account of the lack of a permanent secretarial address. With members acquiring computers in the early to mid-nineties, the production and distribution of documents has been greatly eased. Much of this recent material has been preserved on disc.

In order to make its existence more widely known, the Group was listed for many years in the Flight Directory of British Aviation (no longer published). In addition, a reference to the Group was placed in the May 1989 edition of the Directory of British Associations. This has been updated in subsequent editions. While these references have become less important with increasing availability of the internet, they have provided a worthwhile means of enabling the public to contact the Group.

A significant development has been the establishment of the Group's first website late in 1999. The current website can be accessed on `http://www.airsafetygroup.org`.

SOME OTHER GROUPS & ORGANISATIONS PROMOTING SAFETY IN CIVIL AIR TRANSPORT

The question has sometimes been asked: was it really necessary to form a new group at all? Were not existing groups tackling, or capable of tackling, the same concerns? This question was faced by the founders at the outset. The answer was a reluctant 'no', at least with regard to the jet fuel issue. Furthermore, the constitution of the Group was, and remains, such that its sole concern is the safety of passengers in civil transport aircraft. Nevertheless, it has always been the Group's declared aim, while maintaining its independence, to liaise with other safety and accident prevention organisations and other aviation societies not specifically related to safety.

In this context the Group acknowledges the impartial research carried out by the technical committees/working parties of a number of associations. While formal liaisons with such bodies have not been made (with one exception; see below), future developments may indicate the desirability of closer collaboration between all safety-related groups.

It is worth listing such groups, with some of which the Group has enjoyed intermittent but cordial relations over many years. Much of the information given below is available on-line and from other sources. The list does not include statutory bodies.

UK Flight Safety Committee (UKFSC)

This was founded in 1959 initially to address concerns about the UK safety record at the time. Through its regular meetings it provided, and continues to provide, a forum for confidential discussion and exchange of information between regulators, operators, manufacturers, professional bodies, trade associations and insurers. The Committee has developed over the years, some 90 or more organisations, both UK and international, being currently represented. The organisation is financed by subscriptions from its various members. The Committee's activities are published in a quarterly magazine: "FOCUS on Commercial Aviation Safety".

A number of ASG members have been members also of the UKFSC

Air Transport Users Council (AUC)

This is the UK's consumer council for air transport. It was established at the time of the formation of the Civil Aviation Authority in April 1972 and is included within the CAA corporate structure. It is funded by the CAA, its remit being to assist the CAA in furthering "the reasonable interests of users of air transport services". While safety is within the remit, most of the AUC's activities have been to do with other concerns of air travellers. The Council's chairman and members are appointed by, but may not be members of, the CAA. Members are appointed as individuals and not as delegates of other groups.

Parliamentary Advisory Council for Transport Safety (PACTS)

This is a registered charity and company limited by guarantee, its charitable objective being "to protect human life through the promotion of transport safety for the public benefit". It is an associate Parliamentary Group established to advise and inform members of the Commons and Lords on air, road and rail safety. It organises periodic conferences including the annual Westminster Lecture on transport safety. It has a number of working parties, the aviation one having been chaired by members of the ASG (though acting as individuals and not representing the ASG). PACTS is a founder member of the European Transport

Safety Council (ETSC) (See below). Its income is derived from subscriptions, sponsorship, event income and research funding.

The ASG is pleased to record that in 2008 a Memorandum of Understanding between itself and PACTS was signed whereby the ASG provides, as required, aviation safety advice to the Council. Joint ASG/PACTS meetings are held two or three times a year at Portcullis House.

International Airline Passengers Association (IAPA)

This organisation grew out of the US-founded Airways Club referred to earlier in this history. In the mid-sixties it changed its name to the Airline Passengers Association, and later to the current name of International Airline Passengers Association. As already recorded, fruitful collaboration occurred between the ASG and the Airways Club at about the time of the ASG's formation. This collaboration was significant in reversing the trend towards the use of Jet B fuel. While safety issues are an important part of the organisation's remit, its principal activity is obtaining for its members the best available rates for insurance, hotels, car rental, and the provision of travel planning and other information of assistance to the frequent traveller. The Association has a large worldwide membership. In recent years IAPA's safety concerns were overseen by one of the UK's prominent safety consultants, the late Ronald Ashford, who was also a member of the ASG.

Flight Safety Foundation (FSF)

This is an independent, impartial, non-profit organisation, and is probably the best known of the non-statutary bodies. It was founded in 1947 in the United States by Jerome F Lederer for the purpose of promoting continuous improvement in global aviation safety. This is achieved through research, auditing, education, advocacy and publishing. It has an international membership in excess of 1200 organisations and individuals in 150 countries. The FSF organises seminars in various parts of the world. Its activities are published in a monthly magazine: "AeroSafety World".

International Federation of Airworthiness (IFA)

This body evolved in the early sixties from the Society of Licenced Aircraft Engineering Technologists (SLAET), its emphasis being on maintenance engineering. Its first name was the International Federation of Aircraft and Technology and Engineering, this being changed in 1975 to the current name of International Federation of Airworthiness. Quoting from its website, it is "dedicated to improving aviation safety by increasing international communication, awareness and cooperation on all airworthiness issues and particularly that of continuing airworthiness." As the organisation developed, it acquired the status of a Non-Governmental Organisation (NGO), with an international membership, including many distinguished names, from airlines, manufacturers, repair agencies, regulatory authorities and professional societies. The Federation holds technical seminars which, on occasions, are in conjunction with, and hosted by, other organisations. In 2004 ICAO admitted the Federation to membership of its Airworthiness Panel.

Aviation Study Group

This group was founded in 1992 by the late Dr James Vant (not a medical doctor) and Derek Dempster. Vant had previously been a prominent member of the ASG. One of the long term objectives of the Study Group has been the establishment of a Chair of Aviation Safety and an Institute of Aviation Safety Management, both at the University of Oxford. Pending the accomplishment of these longer-term aims, the group's remit has differed little from that of the ASG. The group is centred at Linacre College, Oxford. It has extensive contacts within the aviation world, and was able to recruit an impressive list of distinguished members from the world-wide aviation community, perhaps the most notable being Dr Assad Kotaite, past President of the Council of ICAO, and the Hon Carl Vogt, former Chairman of the US NTSB. The group is funded by membership subscriptions, sponsorship and donations from benefactors. Since its formation, a number of one-day seminars have been hosted by the group in Oxford.

It is unfortunate that the Aviation Study Group has the same initials (ASG) as the ASG which is the subject of this history. This has caused much confusion and has sometimes led to the two groups being unofficially designated as ASG (Oxford) and ASG (Westminster) respectively.

The safety concerns of the two groups have been virtually identical.

European Transport Safety Council (ETSC)

As already noted, PACTS was one the founder-members of this Brussels-based council which was founded in 1993. Its purpose is to provide impartial advice on transport safety issues to the European Commission, Parliament and member States. It is funded from a variety of sources.

ETSC has a number of aviation safety working groups on which ASG member Frank Taylor, in his Cranfield capacity, has served for several years. Information deriving from ETSC's researches is promulgated in various publications. In addition, it organises several conferences annually, including the European Transport Safety Lecture. By an arrangement with PACTS, ASG member Capt Roberts has attended joint EASA, ESSI & ECAST meetings in Cologne on behalf of the ETSC.

Survivors Campaign to Improve Safety in Airline Flight Equipment (SCISAFE)

Following some accidents, members of the public, some of whom may have been on board the subject aircraft, and/or have lost relatives or friends in the accidents, have formed pressure groups to improve safety. One such group is SCISAFE which was formed following the B737 accident at Manchester in 1985. The founders of this group felt that the requirements relating to emergency evacuation and cabin safety generally were unsatisfactory. Their concerns are shared by the ASG with whom the new group has been in contact over the years since that accident.

A further such group, known as the Air Safety Action Group, was formed as a result of the B737 accident at Kegworth in 1989. Its remit was to draw attention to safety deficiencies brought to light by that accident.

Royal Aeronautical Society (RAeS)

This is the foremost aviation society in the United Kingdom. It has many working parties and hosts numerous lectures and symposia. There has been informal contact over the years between the Group and the Society. Many Group members are members of the Society in its various grades.

Institution of Mechanical Engineers (IMechE)

This is one of the most prominent professional engineering societies. It has an Aerospace Industries Division which arranges conferences, seminars and lectures, and also co-sponsors events with the Royal Aeronautical Society and other organisations.

International Society of Air Safety Investigators (ISASI)

The forerunner body, the Society of Air Safety Investigators, was founded in the United States in 1964, its purpose being to promote safety through the exchange of information derived from accident investigations. By 1977 membership had increased to 100 individual members from 35 countries, the name then being changed to the present one in order to reflect its international status. Affiliated societies are located in many parts of the world.

As already noted, a number of ASG members are members also of ISASI.

Guild of Air Pilots and Air Navigators (GAPAN) Technical and Air Safety Committee

The Guild was founded in 1929, its aim being to establish and maintain the highest standards of air safety through the promotion of good airmanship. The Guild became a City of London Livery Company in 1956. A number of Group members have been/are Liverymen, two having also been Masters of the Guild.

The Technical and Air Safety Committee handles all aspects of safety: it makes submissions to the Authorities and prepares contributions to conferences and the House of Commons Select Committee on Transport.

British Airline Pilots Association (BALPA) Flight Safety Committee

This group has for many years been engaged in well researched work on various safety issues. There has been informal liaison between it and the ASG.

House of Commons Select Committee on Transport

This committee's remit is to examine the expenditure, administration and policy of the Department for Transport and its associated public bodies. Its inquiries cover road, rail and air transport.

Clearly, when addressing matters of aviation safety, the deliberations of this committee are of interest to the Group. In 1989, the Group made a written submission when the committee was inquiring into aircraft cabin safety. This submission was later referenced in the committee's report. When, ten years later, the committee was again inquiring into aviation safety, the Group was not officially informed, and hence lost the opportunity of making a submission. Subsequent investigation revealed that, possibly on account of administrative mishandling within the Commons, the Group's name had not been on the current list of bodies to be kept informed. This omission has been rectified, all subsequent inquiries being notified to the Group.

ASG and PACTS submitted a joint memorandum in 2009 to the committee's inquiry into airspace capacity, and also gave oral evidence.

Universities

While there are several universities which grant degrees in aviation subjects, the Group has had regular contact with only one, namely, the University of Cranfield. This liaison has been of an informal kind, resulting from the fact that a Group founder member, Frank Taylor, has spent much of his career there.

Group members have given occasional lectures at the university and one of the Group's Chairmen, Capt Pritchard, participated in the university's accident investigation courses over a period of 22 years. Two other Group members, John Lodge and Robert Belton also lectured at many of these courses.

In recognition of its long association with the university, the Group is sponsoring a shield to be awarded annually to the graduate who, in the opinion of the university, has written the best thesis on a safety-related subject. The first such presentation was made in June 2009 to Marie Michalkova, an MSc graduate.

THE FUTURE

Over the 45 years of the ASG's existence, air transport has come to be acknowledged as a safe and reliable means of transport, this achievement having been brought about by the dedication and professionalism of many who work in the industry and its regulating authorities. In view, however, of the regulatory changes referred to earlier, and of the necessity for aviation to respond to environmental concerns, many potential safety challenges lie ahead. The ASG and other monitoring organisations, working together when appropriate, are assured of a continuing role.

APPENDIX 1

This appendix lists a number of the Group's concerns current in December 2009[1].

Flight Time Limitations

Following a report by Group Captain Douglas Bader in 1975, the first edition of CAP 371-Avoidance of Excessive Fatigue in Aircrews-was introduced by the Civil Aviation Authority. This has stood the test of time over 34 years and is currently in its 4th edition. It can claim to be the world's most comprehensive and up-to-date flight time limitations (FTL) scheme, being based on medical and scientific research.

With the European Aviation Safety Agency (EASA) now responsible for all EU civil aviation, EU OPS 1 Subpart Q was introduced by EASA in July 2008 as the EU-wide FTL regulation. It was basically derived from the JAA Subpart Q work done in the mid-1990s, but which was never formally agreed. As this new scheme, at the time of introduction, was considered by the UK and a number of other EU States to set standards well below those required by their current legislation, EASA issued a derogation permitting the UK to continue using CAP 371 and for other States to continue using their current schemes if more restrictive than Subpart Q. This arrangement is due to terminate in April 2012 when a revised Subpart Q is due to take effect. It is feared, however, that the revised Subpart Q may still not have reached the safety standard evident in CAP 371(4th edition). But if the new Subpart Q is generally acceptable, then all States will have to comply and their individual schemes will be superseded.

[1]Some of the information contained in this Appendix did not become available until early in 2010.

Over the next two years, great efforts will be required by the Group and other concerned parties to ensure that the necessary amendments to Subpart Q will provide a satisfactory standard to allow it safely to supersede CAP 371.

EASA are due shortly to establish Task 055 Working Group to review and revise Subpart Q.

Fuel Tank Flammability

Since 1990 there have been three fuel tank explosions in Boeing aeroplanes engaged in airline operations, two occurring in B737s on the ground, and one in a B747 in flight. The underlying problem has been the relatively high flammability of the vapour space in nominally empty centre tanks, this arising from heat generated by air conditioning equipment located in close proximity to the tanks. On rare occasions when an ignition source is present, explosions can occur. After the tragic loss of the B747 (TWA 800) over Long Island in 1996, the US National Transportation Safety Board (NTSB) urged the Federal Aviation Administration (FAA) to introduce new rules to reduce tank flammability. In due course, the FAA, in 2008, issued a Final Rule on the subject.

This new rule makes a number of provisions including a requirement to limit tank flammability in all newly designed aeroplanes required to be certificated in the US. Another provision requires that modifications be made to reduce tank flammability on the existing US fleets of Boeing 737s and 747s. These new requirements were published by the FAA in its National Operating Requirements rather than in the more usual Airworthiness Directive format.

The International Civil Aviation Organisation (ICAO) recommends that mandatory design and continuing airworthiness information relating to particular types be passed by the State of Design to all other States in which such types are understood to be operated. This is normally achieved by the issue of Airworthiness Directives which, although mandatory only in the State of Design, must be carefully considered by the other States. In the case in question, the FAA appears not to have followed this procedure: there is thus a possibility that the desired safety improvements may not be adopted in all other States where B737s and 747s are operated.

The Air Safety Group's concern has been notified to the FAA, NTSB, ICAO and EASA.

EASA has replied to the effect that a Notice of Amendment (NPA) is being prepared.

Aircraft Maintenance Engineers Working Hours

It has long been recognised that working in a fatigued state increases the risk of errors which, in the aviation context, can result in a reduction in safety. To counter this tendency, flight crews have limitations imposed on their hours of work as well as time taken off between duty periods. Aircraft Maintenance Engineers (AMEs), however, have no specific regulation of their hours of work and are often required to do varying combinations of shift patterns. In addition, some AMEs, when given the opportunity, and for financial gain, are known voluntarily to work 80 or 90 hours a week for several weeks at a time. In some cases this practice can be in contravention of the UK Air Navigation Order which makes it an offence knowingly to work whilst unfit to do so.

Public domain evidence of specific fatigue related maintenance is hard to find, possibly because ICAO Annex 13 (Accident Investigation) does not require AME working hours to be formally recorded. Many UK Accident and Incident reports, however, do cite night shift working and staff shortages as contributory factors.

Following from the above, the ASG has been working with other stakeholders towards achieving a regulatory solution. Initially, the EU Working Time Directive (WTD), which specifies a working week as consisting of no more than 48 hours, was thought to provide a possible solution, although further research suggested that the directive itself was overly simplistic and prescriptive. It was found, however, that the UK has obtained a derogation from this directive, thus allowing the continuance of an unregulated length of the working week. The continuance of the UK derogation is of concern to the ASG, and letters seeking clarification have been sent to EASA and to MEPs. Possible implications of the EU Lisbon Treaty are also being explored.

The ASG has reviewed published data and reports relating to maintenance practices issued by the CAA and ICAO, and has noted the views expressed on various websites. Meetings have been held with senior personnel from maintenance organisations, as well as with the CAA and CHIRP. Initiatives such as Fatigued Risk Management Systems recently put in place by other regulatory authorities, such as Transport Canada, have also been investigated

The ultimate aim of the above research is to promote regulation which will reduce the potential for fatigue related incidents/accidents.

Co-Pilot Line Training

For some years many of those aspiring to a career as pilots in civil aviation have had to self-finance their training in order to obtain basic qualifications. Syllabuses specifying technical courses, simulator flying and base flying have been established by regulation in order to ensure that prospective professional pilots have achieved the necessary minimum standards to qualify for various type ratings. This is achieved by licensing of the training establishments, and includes the approvals of Training Captains and Type Rating and Instrument Rating examiners.

There is, however, one aspect of training which falls outside the control of the regulatory authorities. This is 'line training' in the course of which airlines' training captains supervise less experienced, though type rated, pilots over sometimes prolonged periods to ensure that they are brought up to a standard at which they become fully suited for employment on the airlines' route structures, and with any captain. This line training is routinely carried out with fare-paying passengers on board and, in the case of two-crew aircraft, inevitably results in some, though usually small, reduction in overall safety margins.

Of greater concern is that a market has developed in which 'freelance' pilots pay an airline to provide them with line training, although such pilots are unlikely to become employed by those airlines and may not, therefore, be subject to their standards and disciplines. This practice provides financial rewards for the airlines concerned and also enables them to reduce their number of 'in house' pilots. Such training of 'freelance' pilots is conducted with passengers on board, and the ASG considers that, in some cases, safety margins may be compromised to an unacceptable degree. The Group considers that line training of 'freelance' pilots should be subject to regulatory oversight.

This matter has been brought to the attention of EASA and the CAA.

Mobile Telephone Use in flight

The use of mobile phones in flight was banned in the mid-nineties. The ban was introduced on account of numerous incidents of interference between phone transmissions and aircraft systems, this resulting in false inputs to both flight and engine control systems, and also to navigation systems.

New systems have now been developed which make use of 'pico cells' installed in the aircraft. These allow interference-free communication between mobile phones and ground stations, but only above 10000 ft. Only a limited number of phones, however, can be accommodated by such systems at any one time. This limitation will need to be handled by the cabin crew.

On older, unmodified, aircraft the ban on mobile phones will need to remain. This in turn may result in increased frustration among some members of the travelling public who have begun to consider voice communication as a right.

The Group's concerns are threefold: firstly, whether an acceptable level of reliability of the modified phone systems can be achieved in preventing interference with aircraft systems; secondly, whether, with modified systems, cabin crews will be able to manage passengers unable to use their phones; and, thirdly, whether passengers will exhibit unacceptable behaviour if their use of phones is prohibited in either modified or unmodified aircraft.

These matters have been brought to the attention of the EU and UK Authorities and these have been acknowledged. EASA has subsequently supplied a report, ED 130 issued in December 2006 by EUROCAE, that provides guidance for the use of portable electronic devices on board aircraft.

Misuse of Lasers

High-powered hand-held laser devices have for some time been available for purchase by the general public. The Group monitors closely the growing global trend for such devices to be misused and their beams targeted at aircraft usually on approach to or departure from an airport. This foolhardy and potentially dangerous practice appears to be increasing exponentially, incidents being reported from all over the world .In the UK many such incidents have been reported to the CAA by pilots and controllers by means of the Mandatory Occurrence Report (MOR) system.

The Group is pleased to acknowledge that the CAA has initiated a new law which makes the above practice a criminal offence. This has been done by the introduction of Article 222 to the Air Navigation Order 2009. The new Article states that: "A person must not in the United Kingdom direct or shine any light at an aircraft in flight so as to dazzle or distract the pilot of the aircraft." This will come into effect on 1st January 2010. It is expected that police helicopter units, using new technology, will be increasingly involved in tracking offenders.

The issue of laser misuse was referred by the Group to EASA in mid-2009. It is not yet known whether the UK's new law will be adopted by the Agency and made applicable to other EC States.

Cabin Air Quality

A debate on cabin air quality has been going on for some decades, but perhaps more especially in the past 20 years or so during which tobacco smoking in airliners has been progressively banned. The debate derives from the fact that cabin air in most turbine-powered aircraft is supplied by air bled from the engine compressors. On occasions this bleed air can be contaminated in varying degrees by engine oil, and this can result in ill-effects on crew and passengers. The first recorded case occurred in 1977 when a C130 Hercules navigator became incapacitated in flight following a 'fume event'. At about the same time, some cases were reported of pilots of a particular type of military aircraft feeling unwell as a result of exposure to contaminated bleed air. The solution in these latter cases lay in the installation of carbon activated filters. In less severe cases of contamination, however, ill-effects may not be immediately apparent but can surface after years of exposure to low concentrations of fumes which may not be detectable by sight or smell.

The ill-effects referred to above became known as 'Aerotoxic Syndrome', the term being coined in 1999 by US, Australian and French researchers.

Studies have been carried out by government-funded and independent organisations, but with varied results. While all parties accept that oil fumes can have an acute and irritant effect, the issue of chronic health effects is still hotly contested, the aviation industry maintaining that there is insufficient evidence to link long-term health effects with oil fumes. Independent campaign groups, however, such as the Aerotoxic Association(AA), the Global Cabin Air Quality Executive (GCAQE) and the Aviation Organophosphate Information Service(AOPIS) have a different view. These groups have gathered a wealth of evidence, including testimonies from prematurely retired (on medical grounds) crew members, that contaminated air has undoubtedly been causing long-term health problems. In the light of this evidence, the campaigning groups have long been advocating that the authorities should require, and that industry should implement, remedial measures to mitigate the problem of the Syndrome.

In response to pressure from the above groups, and, independently, from the ASG, EASA, has recently invited submissions from all interested parties. Accordingly, the campaigning groups have provided the Agency with data accumulated over the past three years. No definitive response has yet been received, though it is understood that this evidence will be reviewed over the next year.

In 2007 the House of Lords Select Committee on Science and Technology investigated Aerotoxic Syndrome. One of the committee's recommendations was that further research be carried out into the chemicals and their concentrations present in oil fumes. This research is being done by Cranfield University whose findings are expected in March 2010.

APPENDIX 2

This appendix comprises a copy of the minutes of the Group's formation meeting in December 1964.

AIR SAFETY GROUP

Minutes of Formation Meeting held on Tuesday, 8th December, 1964, at 7.00 p.m. at The Royal Aero Club.

Present:	Mr. H. Morris	Acting Chairman
	Mrs. Cox	
	Mr. F. Taylor	
	Mr. D. Wakeling	
	Mr. E.L. Bass	
	Mr. A. Piercy	
	Mr. G.C. Scott	
	Mr. J.W. Rickard	
	Mr. J. Tye) Mr. Lamb) Mr. P. Love)	British Safety Council
	Mr. Craddock) Mr. J.E. Lodge)	National Association of Fire Officers
	Mr. R.C. Neve	Observer on behalf of BALPA
	Mr. J.S. Carter	Guild of Travel Writers
	Mr. J. Ramsden	Flight International
	Mr. R. Mariner	Institute of Travel Managers in Commerce and Industry
	Mr. H.W. Payne	Society of Licensed Aircraft Engineers and Technologists
	Mr. D. St. B. Sladen	London Chamber of Commerce
	Dr. J. Wedgwood	Observing on behalf of BMA

Organisations wishing to be informed of developments were:-

Federation of British Industries
Association of British Travel Agents
London Tourist Board
Institution of Professional Civil Servants
British Institute of Management
British Medical Association

Mr. Eric Lubbock was to have taken the chair, but was unfortunately prevented from attending by his Parliamentary duties. It had previously been arranged that Mr. Morris would chair the meeting in the absence of Mr. Lubbock.

1. With regard to the exploratory meeting held on 19th October, Mr. Rickard stated that the outcome of this had been reported in the letter issued by Mr. Tye, Controller, British Safety Council, representative of the Ad Hoc Committee, on 30th October, of which all present had copies. However, in response to questions, Mr. Morris and Mr. Rickard elaborated on certain points.

2. The meeting was convened by Mr. Tye on behalf of the Ad Hoc Committee.

3. After some discussion it was agreed that the title AIR SAFETY GROUP should be retained.

4. It was agreed that there would be no constitution nor qualification for membership at this stage, that the whole Group would form a committee meeting quarterly.

5. It was proposed by James Tye, seconded by J. Rickard and passed that Mr. Morris should act as joint Chairman of the Group with Mr. Lubbock (Mr. Lubbock to be approached by Mr. Rickard).

6. It was further proposed by Mr. Morris, seconded by Mr. Piercy and unanimously agreed, that Mr. Rickard should act as Honorary Secretary to the Group. The Group's temporary address would be: c/o The British Safety Council, 163/173 Praed Street,, London, W.2.

7. The object of the Group - to promote greater safety for air travellers. It is not intended to duplicate work at present being done by the existing airworthiness authorities and other professional bodies, but rather to fill in the gaps and tackle those issues which are not at present receiving adequate treatment.

8. In order to cover initial expenses, stationary etc., the British Safety Council had donated £20.

9. Of the eight organisations present at the meeting, five wished to be associated immediately with the work of the Group. The representatives of the remaining three possessed no mandate to commit their organisations. The proposal for association would be referred back and the Group informed as soon as possible.

A decision is also awaited from the following organisations not represented but who were present at the exploratory meeting on 19th. October. The Merchant Navy & Airline Officers Association, Royal College of Surgeons, The Aeroplane and Commercial Aviation News.

10. Of the eight individuals who attended in a purely private capacity, their names may not be used publicly without prior permission, with the exception of those of the Chairman and Honorary Secretary.

11. It was proposed by J. Tye, seconded by J. Rickards and agreed that the object could best be achieved by setting up a number of Working Parties. These were as follows:

12. Fuels: Messrs. Jass, Wakeling and Rickard.

13. Escape and Survival: Messrs. Morris, Craddock and Lodge. Mr. Richard pointed out this subject was very much the concern of Mr. Townshend who, unfortunately, was unable to be present. He would be asked, however, if he would be willing to serve on this Working Party.

14. Air Traffic Control: Messrs. Lamb, Payne and Love.

15. Pilots Working Hours: Mrs. Cox. It is hoped that this subject will appeal also to Dr. Preston who was not present. Mr. Rickard agreed to approach Dr. Preston and suggest that he collaborate with Mrs. Cox.

The subject of crash injuries was also discussed but it was not possible to appoint a Working Party at this stage, mainly on account of the fact that the BMA have not so far committed themselves to collaboration with the Group. Again, this subject may be of interest to Dr. Preston.

Each Working Party would produce a report which would be considered by the committee as a whole before publication of findings and recommendations.

Mr. Lubbock's advice would be sought to enlist support of M.Ps. of all parties and if possible to brief M.Ps.

16. After the meeting a Press statement was produced by Messrs. Tye and Ramsden.

17. The next meeting would be held at 7 p.m. on Tuesday, 16th March at a venue to be advised.

Issued by:- James Tye
British Safety Council
163/173 Praed Street,
London, W.2.

Tel: AMBassador 2415/9.

www.ingramcontent.com/pod-product-compliance
Ingram Content Group UK Ltd.
Pitfield, Milton Keynes, MK11 3LW, UK
UKHW051135260726
13967UKWH00010B/3071